D1129496

JOSEF HERMAN

DRAWINGS

JOSEF HERMAN
Drawings

INTRODUCTION BY BASIL TAYLOR

JONATHAN CAPE

THIRTY BEDFORD SQUARE · LONDON

FIRST PUBLISHED 1956

NC
1115
.H4
T3

E. THAHY
LOYOLA
UNIVERSITY
MEMORIAL LIBRARY

WITHDRAWN

TEXT PRINTED IN GREAT BRITAIN
IN THE CITY OF OXFORD AT THE ALDEN PRESS
ILLUSTRATIONS PRINTED BY JOHN SWAIN & CO. LTD., LONDON
BOUND BY A. W. BAIN & CO. LTD., LONDON

INTRODUCTION BY BASIL TAYLOR

(In this introduction I have gratefully used excerpts from a written statement by the artist as these are not only modest but singularly relevant, lucid and self-aware. The words in inverted commas are therefore Herman's, except where another authorship is indicated.)

JOSEF HERMAN'S work, both as a draughtsman and a painter, has one theme: Man as Labourer and the surroundings of his working life, his home, his family, his landscape. It is a theme which he has discovered in the mining village of Ystradgynlais near Swansea where he lived for ten years from 1944, after settling in Scotland in 1940, in Israel and in the vineyards of Burgundy. The theme is stated without political or sentimental intention and belongs closely to his experience. His father having been a cobbler in Warsaw, he knew from childhood the reality of manual work and the first group of pictures he exhibited in Poland 'in style a vague kind of expressionism, were of peasant life and of the city's industrial suburbs'. He is not a picturesque topographer of working life. 'Neither the Welsh miner nor the Scottish fisherman nor the Burgundian peasant have any interest for me as representative of particular industries. But it is in the study of their appearance that I find the very force of our human destiny bound to labour.' And so the theme, an invitation to sententiousness, is presented with the matter-of-factness of Courbet's *Stone Breakers* or the peasant pictures of Brueghel; the conditions of art and public response in the middle of the twentieth century, when any part of human life may be painted on any scale without disturbance, do not therefore transform his unassertive interests into a manifesto. He does not, as a Courbet, have to defend his right to present life-size and in a public place such a group of miners as his excellent mural in the South Bank exhibition, but for all that the idea possesses him

5

passionately and the bearing of it is suggested by some words he has quoted from the writings of Lionello Venturi. 'It is necessary to go back to Goya, Daumier, Cezanne and Van Gogh in order to remember that in the nineteenth century moral beauty has been identified with the lot of the common people as a reaction against physical beauty, which had by tradition been associated with the upper classes.'

It is proper to make a book from Herman's drawings alone to the exclusion of his paintings, for he has said that 'forming and drawing is the province of ideas and to these I am bound more than to colour'. At a time when so many different kinds of drawings are exhibited and published, when every scrap from the studio floor is liable to be retrieved, catalogued and indexed in somebody's interest, it is necessary to stress the nature of the works reproduced in this book. Almost every one is self sufficient; we are not here peeping behind the scenes, for these drawings are not experiments, trials or preparations except in the sense that any work by a serious artist is undertaken with some degree of speculation and uncertainty. There are other drawings, in pencil, preparatory to these and which Herman does not exhibit. Like the little oil sketches of Constable, they are used to catch and stabilize visual experiences when the eye is alert, the mind not too operative perhaps, the sensibility warm and receptive. The exhibited and published drawings are made in the studio often from the evidence of the first; they represent a development from the original experience and are shaped by the artist's knowledge of physical structures, his manual control and that interior image of his theme which belongs to him uniquely.

Every significant artist carries within his consciousness moulds into which his experience is impressed; from them emerge that image which defies the historian of style with all his descriptive instruments, which is more important than the conscious originality obtained by technical expedients or any shrewd combination of borrowings, that true source of personality which distinguished a

6

Watteau from a Lancret, a Gainsborough from a Reynolds. The form of these internal moulds, as I have crudely described them, is determined by the artist's physical and psychological self, by his sturdiness or frailty, solidity or lightness, quickness or stolidity, by his habit of introversion or extraversion and by a host of other qualities even less easily identified, weighed and measured. What is the image of Man the Labourer which emerges from Herman's mould? He is something sturdy, rooted, a creature in which both stability and energy, gravity and liveliness are balanced; in the description of his physique, weight and the exertion of weight is important, his outline is abrupt, his shape chunky, without being aggressive; he displaces air, treads the ground, clenches his fist, shoulders his spade without rhetoric or the urge to conquer. In this he reflects Herman's own presence, his energy, good humour and physical expressiveness.

Drawing the figure demands physical confidence, an appreciation and experience of the body's complex activity. Also, unlike the writing down of words or music, it finds its quality from the nervous vitality — or paralysis — of the hand's movements and responses. The hand must be a controlled and decisive transmitter of powerful impulses. Herman draws the human figure with the whole of his own body, its past as well as its present condition.

Herman's implements are line and wash, the most elementary means of draughtsmanship, and he uses them with a transparent simplicity as a means of making marks and of laying on paper luminous areas of tone, avoiding the temptation accepted by so many English artists to weaken, or in some cases to disguise weaknesses in, form by playing games with the materials. Herman's line has the same quality as his masses, a certain blunt and weighty directness which seems to incise the paper in the way that his volumes eat into the space. His line is as efficient as a spade and like a good tool its value is functional, the purpose being to express 'the total gravity and strength of a closed mass' and at the same time 'to realize the true proportion of feeling'. (Those who would too

7

casually call him an expressionist should consider the last four words.) The utility of a tool cannot be judged merely by looking at it; it must be taken in hand. Herman's line must not be measured against any ideal of formal or linear beauty but against our personal experience of physical action, pulse and pressure. Like all good drawing it not only contains the artist's ideas and feelings, but summons the bodily and spiritual energies of a responsive spectator.

The areas of wash are no less functional than the line. At one time earlier in his career, Herman enjoyed demonstrating that dramatic glamour which can be had by dexterously combining suggestive veils of ink or watercolour, a method in which Constantin Guys, for example, was so adept, but which must diminish that firm thrust and gravity which he really desires. Now his washes are more solid and less complicated and 'sensitive'; the drama, which he still requires, is in the forms and in the simple contrast of ink and white paper. The design of Herman's pictures, both drawings and paintings, is uncomplicated and stable without being classical in an academic sense; there is no powerful or precisely articulated illusion of space, but the scene is full of air, unconstricted, generously planned. The most forceful movement which the eye is persuaded to follow is downward, not merely to the edge of the paper but into a solid substance of ground. These qualities fulfil his concern for mass 'in its gravitational rather than its plastic sense', of space 'in its poetic rather than its scientific sense', light 'in its dramatic rather than its optical significance'.

Herman is now forty-five. He is an artist of the kind who soon discovers the territory which really possesses his intellectual and emotional allegiance and who then, with a slow and modest certitude, moves towards its conquest. It is an attitude well expressed by another artist of the same type, Georges Braque, when he said that his aim was 'to bring painting within the reach of my own gifts'. It would be no encouragement to such serious and devoted men to suggest that at the age of forty-five either the image they seek to externalize or drawing itself is yet within their grasp.

8

BIBLIOGRAPHY

T. J. HONEYMAN

Foreword to the catalogue of an Exhibition of Paintings by Josef Herman, Connell's Gallery, Glasgow, October 1941.

PHILIP HENDY

Art, New Subjects for Old.
Britain Today, June 1948.

DAVID BELL

The Art of Josef Herman.
The Welsh Review, Summer, 1948.

Miners at Ystradgynlais: Paintings, Pastels and Drawings by Josef Herman. Foreword to the catalogue of the exhibition arranged by the Arts Council of Great Britain, 1948.

ROBERT VRINAT

Josef Herman — Peintre du Peuple de la Mine.
L'Age Nouveau, Paris, August 1949.

STEPHEN ANDREWS

Martin Bloch and Josef Herman.
Canadian Art, Summer 1951.

EDITH HOFFMAN

Josef Herman.
Bamoth, Tel-Aviv, March 1953.

MICHAEL MIDDLETON

Josef Herman, The Pitmen's Painter.
The Studio, October 1953.

Foreword to the catalogue of Five Contemporary British Painters, Canada 1952-53.

JOHN BERGER

Josef Herman.
The Burlington Magazine, June 1955.

HELEN KAPP

Introduction to the catalogue of Wakefield City Art Gallery exhibition: Paintings and Drawings, L. S. Lowry and Josef Herman, 1955.

DAVID PIPER

The Light in the Dark.
Broadcast in the B.B.C. Third Programme, reprinted in the *Jewish Quarterly*, Spring 1956.

9

DAVID BAXANDALL	Josef Herman. Foreword to the catalogue of Whitechapel Art Gallery exhibition, March/April, 1956.
CLIFF HOLDEN	Josef Herman. *Paletten* No. 2, Stockholm 1956.
CHARLES S. SPENCER	Josef Herman. Jewish Affairs, Johannesburg, June 1956.
LONA TRUDING	Ein Epos der Erde. *Goetheanum*, August 1956.

BIOGRAPHICAL NOTE

JOSEF HERMAN was born in Warsaw in 1911. He came to England by way of Belgium in 1940 and lived for three years in Scotland where he exhibited in Glasgow and Edinburgh. His first London exhibition was at the Lefevre Gallery in 1943. The following year he settled in the Welsh mining village of Ystradgynlais and there produced his series of paintings and drawings of the mining community. From 1946 onwards he exhibited in London with Roland, Browse & Delbanco. He has travelled widely, all over Europe and Israel. In 1951 he painted a mural for the Festival of Britain, which formed the centre-piece for his large one-man show of paintings and drawings at the Whitechapel Art Gallery in 1956.

Works by Josef Herman are in the following Public Collections:

Aberdeen, Art Gallery
Arts Council of Great Britain
Auckland, N.Z., Art Gallery
Birmingham, Museum and Art Gallery
Bristol, City Art Gallery
Cardiff, National Museum of Wales
Contemporary Art Society
Glasgow, City Art Gallery
Huddersfield, Art Gallery
Leeds, City Art Gallery
Leicester, Museum and Art Gallery
London, Tate Gallery
London, Geffrye Museum
Manchester, City Art Gallery
Melbourne, National Gallery of Victoria, Australia
Montreal, Museum of Fine Arts
Salford, Art Gallery
Southampton, Art Gallery
Swansea, Glynn Vivian Art Gallery
Tel-Aviv, Art Gallery
Toronto, Art Gallery
Wakefield, City Art Gallery

LIST OF PLATES

1 MIKE Size 22½ × 17¼ in. 1945
In the possession of J. Evans, Esq.

2 TWO MINERS WORKING Size 6 × 9 in. 1948
In the possession of Dr. H. Roland

3 TWO KNEELING MINERS AT WORK UNDERGROUND
Size 7⅜ × 9⅜ in. 1948
In the possession of Dr. H. Roland

4 MINER Size 7¾ × 10 in. 1946
Present owner unknown

5 THE SHEEPSHEARERS Size 7 × 9 in. 1947
In the possession of E. Newmark, Esq.

6 HORSES Size 6¼ × 9½ in. 1947
In the possession of Dr. G. Delbanco

7 TOIL Size 7¼ × 10 in. 1946
In the possession of Dr. G. Delbanco

8 THE STONEBREAKER Size 6½ × 9 in. 1948
In the possession of Dr. H. Roland

9 THE MINERS' BRASSBAND Size 9½ × 13¾ in. 1946
In the possession of Dr. H. Roland

10 FISHERMAN AND NETS Size 7 × 10 in. 1948
In the possession of M. Harrison, Esq.

11 LANDSCAPE — UPPER ITALY Size 7½ × 9¾ in. 1949
In the possession of L. Cohen, Esq.

12 PEASANT IN THE FIELD Size 8 × 10 in. 1950
In the possession of S. Andrews, Esq.

13 MOTHER AND CHILD   Size 28½ × 21 in. 1951
          In the possession of Messrs. Gimpel fils.

14 FISHERMEN MENDING THEIR NETS
                              Size 8 × 10 in. 1951
          In the possession of Dr. H. Roland

15 THREE FISHERMEN RESTING   Size 7¾ × 9¾ in. 1951
          In the possession of Sir Philip Hendy

16 LANDSCAPE WITH THREE TREES   Size 7½ × 9¾ in. 1951
          In the possession of G. Dixon, Esq.

17 OLD PEASANT AND HIS WIFE IN THE VINEYARDS
                              Size 8 × 10 in. 1951
          In the possession of Dr. H. Roland

18 THE CARTHORSE   Size 6½ × 9 in. 1953
          In the possession of J. H. Strachan, Esq.

19 LANDSCAPE WITH THREE TREES   Size 8 × 10 in. 1952
          In the possession of Mrs. D. Astor

20 PRUNING THE VINE   Size 8 × 10 in. 1951
          In the possession of Dr. H. Roland

21 YEMENITE GIRL   Size 8 × 10 in. 1952
          In the possession of Miss L. Browse

22 ISRAELI LANDSCAPE   Size 6¾ × 9 in. 1952
          In the possession of Mr. K. Strauss

23 TWO STANDING MINERS   Size 9 × 6¾ in. 1953
          In the possession of M. Halperin, Esq.

24 TWO MEN ON A BENCH   Size 7¾ × 9¾ in. 1954
          In the possession of Dr. H. Roland

25 WOMEN ON THE SHORE   Size 8 × 10 in. 1953
          In the possession of Mrs. C. Herman

26 BACK OF SQUATTING NUDE   Size 9 × 6¾ in. 1953
          In the possession of the Artist

27 STANDING NUDE   Size 9 × 6¾ in. 1953
          In the possession of D. L. Sandelson, Esq.

28 MAN IN DOORWAY WITH DOG   Size 9 × 6¾ in. 1953
      In the possession of the Manchester City Art Gallery

29 STUDIES OF MINERS   Size 10 × 8 in. 1954
      In the possession of the Contemporary Art Society

30 IN THE 'MINERS' ARMS'   Size 7½ × 9½ in. 1954
      In the possession of the Tate Gallery, London

31 BURGUNDIAN PEASANT   Size 25 × 20 in. 1953
      In the possession of W. Gardener, Esq.

32 MAN DIGGING   Size 8 × 10 in. 1954
      In the possession of M. Cahn, Esq.

33 CONVERSATION   Size 7¾ × 9¾ in. 1954
      In the possession of the Geffrye Museum, London

34 POTATO DIGGERS   Size 8 × 10 in. 1954
      In the possession of Roland, Browse & Delbanco

35 THREE MINERS AT PITHEAD   Size 8 × 10 in. 1954
      In the possession of D. Matthews, Esq.

36 WALK BY THE SEA   Size 7½ × 9½ in. 1954
      In the possession of E. Loewenstein, Esq.

37 THREE WORKMEN WITH SHOVELS Size 6¾ × 9 in. 1956
      In the possession of M. Halperin, Esq.

38 LUNCHTIME   Size 7½ × 9½ in. 1956
      In the possession of M. Halperin, Esq.

39 TWO MINERS SITTING   Size 7½ × 9½ in. 1956
      In the possession of V. Eagle, Esq.

40 FOUR FISHERMEN   Size 7½ × 9½ in. 1956
      In the possession of H. B. Anderman, Esq.

THE DRAWINGS

MIKE   1945

2　TWO　MINERS　WORKING　　　　　　　　　1948

3　TWO　KNEELING　MINERS　AT　WORK　UNDERGROUND　1948

4 MINER   1946

5   THE SHEEPSHEARERS   1947

6   HORSES   1947

7 TOIL   1946

8   THE STONEBREAKER   1948

9   THE MINERS' BRASS BAND   1946

10 FISHERMAN AND NETS   1948

11 LANDSCAPE – UPPER ITALY   1949

12   PEASANT IN THE FIELD   1950

13 MOTHER AND CHILD   1951

14 FISHERMEN MENDING THEIR NETS   1951

15 THREE FISHERMEN RESTING   1951

16 LANDSCAPE WITH THREE TREES   1951

17   OLD PEASANT AND HIS WIFE IN THE VINEYARDS   1951

18　THE CART-HORSE　　　　　　　　　1953

19　LANDSCAPE WITH THREE TREES　　　　1952

20 PRUNING THE VINE   1951

21 YEMENITE GIRL 1952

22   ISRAELI LANDSCAPE   1952

23   TWO STANDING MINERS   1953

24   TWO MEN ON A BENCH   1954

25 WOMEN ON THE SHORE   1953

26 BACK OF SQUATTING NUDE   1953

27   STANDING NUDE   1953

28 MAN IN DOORWAY WITH DOG   1953

29   STUDIES OF MINERS   1954

30 IN THE "MINERS' ARMS"   1954

31 BURGUNDIAN PEASANT   1953

E. M. CUDAHY
LOYOLA
UNIVERSITY
MEMORIAL LIBRARY

32 MAN DIGGING   1954

33 CONVERSATION   1954

34 POTATO DIGGERS   1954

35   THREE MINERS AT PITHEAD   1954

36 WALK BY THE SEA   1954

37   THREE WORKMEN WITH SHOVELS   1956

38   LUNCHTIME   1956

39   TWO MINERS SITTING   1956

40   FOUR FISHERMEN   1956